The Little Cookie

MW01050501

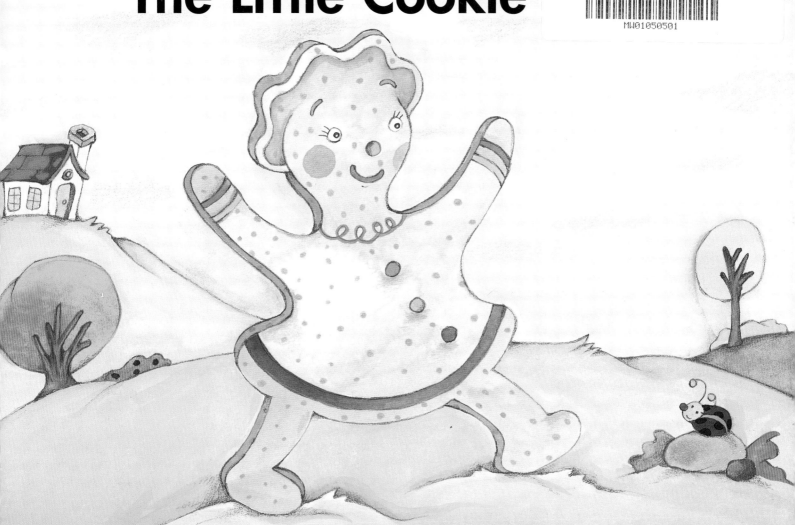

The little cookie girl jumped out.

2

She ran out the door.
She ran and ran.

3

4 **The three little pigs saw the little cookie girl.**

"Come back! Come back!"
said the three little pigs.

6 **The three bears saw the little cookie girl.**

"Come back! Come back!"
said the three bears.

The little cookie girl ran and ran.
She ran up the hill.

Jack and Jill saw the little cookie girl. 9

"Come back!" said Jill.
"Come back!" said Jack.

The little cookie girl ran and ran.
She ran down the hill.

The fox saw the little cookie girl.

The fox saw the three little pigs and the three bears.

The fox saw Jack and Jill.

"Come here! Come here!" said the fox.

We can all have fun here!